Glance at Eternity

Glance at Eternity

One Person's Visit to Eternity,
Beyond Death!

Yosief Tewolde (Seber)

Library of Congress Control Number:		2015908792
ISBN:	Hardcover	978-1-5144-6063-4
	Softcover	978-1-5144-6062-7
	eBook	978-1-5144-6061-0

Email: ucf@iname.com
Twitter: @ucf_seber
Facebook: ucft seber

Cover design by: Abraham Weldeyesus Yohannes

Print information available on the last page.

Rev. date: 07/10/2015

To order additional copies of this book, contact:
Xlibris
800-056-3182
www.Xlibrispublishing.co.uk
Orders@Xlibrispublishing.co.uk
712917

Contents

1. The Glance 3

2. First Hospital 9

3. Second Hospital 13

4. Discharge and Further Treatment through
   a Third Hospital and Rehabilitation...........................15

5. My New Perspective..17

6. Me in My Second Life...23

7. Causes...25

8. What Helped? Saved by the Common Person 27

9. My Takes 29

10. Perspectives of Heaven 33

Foreword

*H*ere is a recount of an episode in my life. Thanks to my family and friends and the spiritualists and medical professionals who have proved good to me and who continue to support me to go forward in my new life.

I also appreciate those that advised me to write the recount of my experience. This is my experience.

My aim is not to profit out of this but to express my feelings and share my experiences. I ask that you look into this from a positive angle. All I ask of you is to remember me in your good wishes.

Thanks to all who supported me in different circumstances. This is my first and hopefully my final glance at eternity.

The cover design, an eye staring at the universe, indicates the medical experience and the new life I entered, following my glimpse at eternity.

It should be noted that this book was written immediately after I was discharged from the hospital on 3 February 2011.

For the blessings I received, I dedicate this work to Maria and Martha.

The Glance

I had a glance at eternity. This is a story about my visit to the afterlife that I encountered . . . Yes, I encountered it, and I am here to tell you how I came out of it. Reaching this level where I can recount what I know about it is mind-boggling.

I am told that having life is a blessing. Well, having reached the stage where I had a glance at eternity, being at the crossroads of returning to life and going the abode of eternity, I should know that by now. My glance and visit of a short duration to eternity, as it may be, was that—a visit and a glance which my recollection has not registered during its progress. I don't know whether that is classed as a lucky or unlucky experience. It certainly was a terrifying and overwhelming encounter. At the same time, it is a blessing to have come back to talk about it.

I never knew it. I never thought before my incident that life is immaculate. When we are alive, we take it for granted, as I did before my glance at eternity. In some instances, I still sometimes take life for granted even after being discharged from the hospital. It is a taken, and it is not considered as a visitation to living life. We are indulgent in life as if we will live forever and it is not just a visit. It happens to be a reality. My experience of having a glance at eternity was to remind me and inform me first-hand that my life is in fact just a visit. I had a glimpse visit to eternity following a drastic incident which I knew absolutely nothing about. I was not aware of it. We do not often think life as something temporary, and as such ending either when involved in it, that is limited and executed differently, limitedly.

Now, I just realized that my first visit to life had been irrelevant. It had ended some months ago or so, I was told by psychologists and my loved ones. I was then discharged from three consecutive big hospitals and from rehabilitation centres. When I found myself on another visit, a second visit, to life, a visitor asked me, 'Would you be able to return your default statures and your disabilities if you were to have a coloured story about your circumstances?' I am not sure.

What is, yes existence, yes life, yes the waking up and the sleeping phenomena, yes encountering, yes enjoyment and sadness as it may well be and as you know it from being in it. These are what I mean by visitation episodes.

I find everything in life new and at odds with the concept I have installed in my head from the last time I encountered it, of course. It was more likely before I fell into this new circumstance.

I was not a witness to the fact that the first visitation had elapsed some time ago. I was told that I should be feeling grateful, and I was told and advised to be grateful that I escaped death and in such a mild state after the episode that initially got me to have a glance at eternity. I only confirmed the outcome of the end of the first visitation by way of an amputated leg, a depreciated eye due to glaucoma, and brain damage. How, when, and on what grounds? It is a blank, as far as I am concerned. Then again, the pieces of advice, like the one above, that were given to me are irrelevant to me as none of my depreciation will be recalibrated or returned to its previous state as confirmed by my health practitioners.

Glaucoma is a term describing a group of ocular (eye) disorders that result in optic nerve damage, often associated with increased fluid pressure in the eye (intraocular pressure) (IOP). The disorders can be roughly divided into two main categories, "open-angle" and "closed-angle" (or "angle closure") glaucoma. Open-angle chronic glaucoma is painless, tends to develop slowly over time and often has no symptoms until the disease has progressed significantly. It is treated with either glaucoma medication to lower the pressure, or with various pressure-reducing glaucoma surgeries. Closed-angle glaucoma, however, is characterized by sudden eye pain, redness, nausea and vomiting, and other symptoms resulting from a sudden spike in intraocular pressure, and is treated as a medical emergency.

Glaucoma can permanently damage vision in the affected eye(s), first by decreasing peripheral vision (reducing the visual field), and then potentially leading to blindness if left untreated.

Apparently and peculiarly, the events in my real-life storyline are but a new entrance and a new depiction into the same life as I encountered it previously.

It seems to me that these new events make me see things from a different light, interpret things on a different relevance, and perceive things on a different scale.

I woke up on my hospital bed. I think it was afternoon. My thinking process took place in a while as I did for some days. At this time, I came to realize that my leg was missing. I didn't have any traceable inkling of memory, and I didn't see any hurting wound or healing wound or bandaged wound to associate it with. I didn't see medical personnel running around to inform me that I do not have a leg, by the way. The thing is, I awoke after a lengthy time of being comatose. The fact is that it was a new story only to me. I was the guest not knowing what was happening. The only person who did not know why I was there or how I got there was only me. I was not even aware I had been there for some months. That was when I worked it out. For others—like the many medical personnel, those who came to visit me, my relatives, my friends, and the community people—it was a shock. For them, it was a long episode that culminated with a lost leg and a damaged brain.

I noticed that I couldn't recognize people—my relatives, friends, and even my children. I couldn't recognize the nurses or understand conversations.

The reality turned out that many who witnessed the amputated leg, the bleeding, the wounds, the patches, and the non-responsive brain squirmed and suffered during the episode with shock and horror. I, who was deep asleep in a coma under intensive care, felt nothing, saw nothing, witnessed nothing. I was not shared with the grief and confusion that befell at those times and days and the joy of my awakening. Am I lucky for having avoided the pain a bit or unlucky for missing the experience? I am not sure if all patients in the hospitals would rather be dead to end their suffering. That is part of its trait or alternatively indulge in the awareness to witness their misery.

As I wrote this, I could not recount any bit of my memory of the time that this supposedly happened, neither a few months around it nor a year around it. The day or the moment of the happening was completely out.

The thing I find fascinating about writing this is not the credit I get in writing or telling a story but as simple as being alive, noting the experience, utilizing what I am called to be grateful for. Although in the event I lost a body part and had other disabilities, I came out of it with a different perspective in life. My challenge would be to define this different perspective.

In recalling events, what most people would say is that it happened at that moment or on that day or during that week or over that month or in that year or any range of timing in that aspect. In my case, none of that has a role—none of it. I cannot relay the whole or part of the story, even those that I would have done in the normal course of life around the particular time. I can just casually state some acts or encounters or events that appear on my mind with a bit of basic details. I can relay happenings of the last few years but could not attach it to any prior or later events. Even when I attempt to relate some stories about that year, I could not do it well. The cause of the event is completely blank and totally rough.

I had taken into account how I found myself now and how I felt and how I was told I had a glance at eternity. Virtually, I had visited eternity or the other side of life for a long time, although I have no memories to back this up with.

Here, I will tell you about my first-hand experiences. These episodes, of course, took place when I found myself awake, following the lengthy time of being comatose as I was informed to have been through by the psychologist and doctor.

In medicine, *coma* is from the Greek word *koma*, meaning 'deep sleep'. It is a profound state of unconsciousness. A comatose patient cannot be awakened, fails to respond normally to pain or light, does not have sleep–wake cycles, and does not take voluntary actions. Coma may result from a variety of conditions, including brain damage due to accident, intoxication, metabolic abnormalities, central nervous system diseases, acute neurologic injuries such as stroke, and hypoxia. It may also be deliberately induced by pharmaceutical agents in order to preserve higher brain function following another form of brain trauma.

First Hospital

*O*ne is never aware when they come out of a coma. In a way, that is to say 'coming back from non-existence to existence'. I was unaware when I went into it or when I came out of it. This is when one would have a glance at eternity. I was told that I had been into a lengthy coma period. I got to the point of going through a therapy and being able to speak and notice. Mine was said to be protracted and medically extended, as if natural comatose was not enough. I cannot say when my eyes opened to see and decipher what was across it or when my ears heard or recognized noise that might have crossed them or when my brain thought what I was doing there or when my body felt and sensed the atmosphere and any pain to announce exiting the comatose period. My visit to eternity came to an end. A new rebirth occurred when I woke up and came back to normality.

Further along, during the conception and rebirth, I could recognize some things which cropped up and crossed my mind, but I could not fully understand what they are even when this was after some weeks of deep sleep following the natural comatose. Other things would be snap pictures of certain episodes with visitors or the staff. It seemed to me that sometimes people were testing my capacity to understand them or testing me if I was following the communication. None of it was clear to me. It was mostly like a dream which one could not decipher or make sense of or relay or recount.

I vaguely remember that at every visit, a particular doctor would ask me questions that you would ask a small child. These were questions like 'What is your name?' 'What is your age?' 'What university did you go to?' or 'What subject did you study in your degree?' It seems to me now on reflection that he was testing my memory capabilities.

Memory is described by psychology as the ability of an organism to store, retain, and subsequently retrieve information. When an individual experiences a traumatic event, whether physically or psychologically traumatic, his or her memory can be affected in many ways.

When people experience physical trauma, such as a head injury in a train accident, this can have effects on their memory. The most common form of memory disturbance in cases of severe injuries or perceived physical distress due to a traumatic event is post-traumatic stress disorder.

Damage to different areas of the brain can have varied effects on memory. The temporal lobes on the sides of the brain contain the hippocampus and amygdala and, therefore, have a lot to do with memory transition and formation.

By one whom I now recognize to be the speech therapist perhaps, I vaguely remember being under an exercise of repeating my name and my date of birth to learn them or relearn them. I certainly succeeded on that as I now fully know those, my name and my date of birth. I was like a small child going to preschool being asked one's name and fully capable of that. Additionally, much of such petty information comes to light. I was like a small five-year-old child brought to attend preschool. While a small child is in a position to answer when asked 'What is your name? How old are you?' I had to learn even that. I felt that being asked 'What is your name?' was well beyond me.

Towards the end in the first hospital, I was able to notice certain things vaguely. I could recognize some people and some of my visitors. Also, I started becoming aware that I was in the hospital, and by then, I recognized some patients and nurses. Also, I knew I was eating fluid concentrates provided for my meals.

I was provided an aid material to urinate and defecate in my bed and was provided liquid food to sip. This progressed to being able to ride the wheelchair to the toilets or to the sitting room, which I utilize now expertly. It is interesting to remember that I could not follow much of what the television was talking about, nor was I able to understand what I read with great difficulty. It was fascinating to find that one time I was able to understand some of the things the TV was saying. That gave me an indication that I probably could somehow read, so I picked up a book from the shelf across. I found that I couldn't read the second sentence without forgetting the first sentence. I couldn't read a paragraph without forgetting the first sentences or the previous paragraph. Having seen a book on my desk, some visitors brought me small books of encouragement, with only a paragraph on a page. I still continue to read them with fondness before retiring to bed.

I have operation marks on my neck and stomach area. Now I have been told that I was breathing through my neck and defecating and urinating through the marks on my belly area.

As I reached this progressive level, I was informed that I would be transferred to another hospital. Afterwards, I remember the nurse stating to me the location of the hospital I would be going to, but I could not understand the directions. I did not know where it was located and the place where it was near to. It was surprising, considering that I knew the place. The nurse mentioned to me that the place near it was somewhere I used to go. This made me think to what extent my memory had been blocked.

Second Hospital

*I*n the second hospital, I was placed in a separate room for medical reasons, it was mentioned to me. To my relatives, I think this was a big episode suggesting that I was more or less out of hospital altogether despite being in another hospital.

My chartered physiotherapist sat me under metal bars reaching my shoulder while I was seated on my wheelchair and fitted strong air-pumped plastic bag on my knees. I was asked to step on it, holding the metal bars. I did, and after a week's practice, I got the hang of it and found myself being promoted to using sticks while inside the bars. Later on, my knee stump was measured by a technician, and a prosthetic leg was manufactured for my need. The newly developed legs replaced the airbags, and I was asked to stand on them with sticks along the metal bars. I have no concept of time, but eventually I worked it out a month later. Supported by the physiotherapists, I was asked to use the sticks provided and try to walk independently about five meters at a time from one section of the practice room to the side. Later on, my walking practice was increased.

My physique seemed to have come up. I was able to keep up my strength, or rather, my physical strength seemed to have sustained. The brain damage was taking more relevance in my case, and my brain memory skills and assessing and analyzing ability seemed to have departed. I found every little thing confusing and oddly placed. All things I saw, deciphered, and analyzed were in place while all the rest are misplaced and improved. As I write this, it seems to me it was.

My main functions at the hospital meant working with psychologists, speech therapists, physiotherapists, and occupational therapists.

Speech therapy meant learning to identify materials from a large book album as indicated by the speech therapist. It was an experience I had not done since I went to year 1 in school. Additionally, to speak and read were my functions. I remember suggesting to the therapist towards the end, if I was told I wouldn't identify by name pictures I was shown, I would have argued. Anyone non-medical person who knew me would argue that I knew all of them, but the reality was not that.

A doctor on the ward would always come to visit me. Beside my bed, he would ask me some simple questions. One day he would ask me 'What is your name?' On another day, he would ask 'Where do you come from?' or 'What are the names of your children?' Now I understand that the whole process was to test my memory level. One day I remember he mentioned to me a story of what happened around my place of origin.

At the end of the week, an occupational therapist would take me on a bus to a supermarket twice with a physiotherapist. It felt like a completely new phenomenon for me to ride a bus and get into a shop. After some similar trips, I was asked to take charge of paying for everyone with the money given and stop the bus when necessary. I remember losing track of what I was meant to do, and I failed to recognize when I had to ring for the stop.

Discharge and Further Treatment through a Third Hospital and Rehabilitation

*A*lthough I was considered to be fit and well, I found the phenomenon to be a challenge. Not knowing what happened to me and how my circumstance had been, further challenges. There were some brief visits, this time under less duress and with good awareness. I was then discharged. Following a relapse, I was considered as mentally unfit. Further on, I recovered, and my mental capacity increased. I was forwarded to a rehabilitation centre. It was a community-based centre where I was rehabilitated well.

There is no single cause for which suicide can be directly attributed. Environmental factors, childhood upbringing, and mental illness each play a large role. Sociologists today consider external circumstances, such as a traumatic event, as a trigger instead of an actual independent cause. Suicides are more likely to occur during periods of socioeconomic, family, and individual crisis. Most people with suicidal tendencies tend to suffer from some mental illness such as depression, bipolar disorder, or some degree of anxiety disorder. These diagnosable mental disorders are associated with more than 90 per cent of suicide victims. As a result, many researchers study the causes of depression to understand the causes of suicide.

My New Perspective

*I*f anything, it would be what perspective I would hold following my retirement period in hospitals and rehabilitation centres.

A few weeks before being discharged from the second hospital, my feeling was not much about my physical and mental hurt, my drawback to life ahead, and my incapacity to face the second life. It was more of a disheartening feeling and concern for the people related to me. They saw the jeopardy and the agony associated with my first encounter. They saw the healing drama, and they agonized over the make-up of it all.

Once released from the hospital, I did morning practice walks, following my practices at the hospital. When I got back from the converted chapel across my apartment which was engaged in and noisily filled with Sunday prayers, I sat in my apartment and meditated. I was consumed by such a thought that went like, 'It is likely that God had to take me on this route. I had to encounter what I encountered and go through a tragic and hefty route possibly because I failed to succumb to the will of God in the simple ways of indulging life.' I found it difficult to scrutinize what the will of God on me might have been, and in part, I found that there were a few scenarios where I failed to fulfil the will of God in me. In short, I possibly have not followed what God intended me to abide by or the functions I was meant to achieve. The encounter was meant as a stoppage of time. It was a time for deep meditation.

What I have to recuperate to move forward from this is my challenge, for which I feel I would need advice from other fellow humans and prayers to God to enlighten me and guide me. A friend told me, 'You survived due to the prayers of the devout Catholic mother you have.'

Thanks to the guiding advice I received from my fellow humans. Noted in my mind are the following:

Accept

A teacher who taught me at some stage had not much to say despite his experience and knowledge in the field. He just suggested to me to *accept* what happened to me. It reverberated in my mind ever since, and I constantly zealously attempt to inscribe it in my brain to make it practically set. It continues to revolve in my mind, noting that my encounter, my drawback, and my disabilities should not be quoted as things better than they are. I have to try to look at it positively, but also I have to accept it. I have to accept it as such, accept it as it is, accept it as drawback, accept it as a disability, and accept it as unpleasant as it is and as it may be.

Not accepting what is real, what my limitations are, and what I face would only leave me with the certainty that I cannot override. For example, without two legs, one would not be able to walk. It would leave the rest of the body hanging on the air as it is not capable to do or handle the task. With only one functioning eye, it is not possible to notice light if the other eye is closed. Simple functionalities and realities call for just acceptance. Moreover, without acceptance, one would only be frustrated, get disappointed, wonder, curse, and continually get angry over the drawback, which will not move or change but will only produce another and further drawnbacks. Simply accepting the reality would enable creativity to take hold and coordinate functionalities of the body.

As I wrote this, I heard a song I had never come across before like the many songs given to me on a memory stick by well-wishers and good people. Among the many others, this was a song by Enya, and it goes like, 'May it be when darkness falls, your heart will be true.' Tears fell from my eyes as I listened to the lyrics of the song. As it ended, I said a prayer.

Having a prosthetic leg made of gold will not change the fact and the reality that there is no leg there. Having eyeglasses made of diamonds does not change the fact about having poor eyesight. This is where the concept of acceptance comes—accepting as it is, accepting what it is, accepting any drawbacks, accepting the whole disability, and accepting every unpleasantness surrounding it. Turning back time, removing the circumstances and the happenings altogether, and changing a subsequent natural make-up are not possible, and they are neither realistic nor practical.

Appreciation

An elderly man who had heard about my situation told me that I should be grateful of my outcome. That is to say that I am lucky, having escaped death, and in this scenario, despite the physical limitations, I should be thankful. It would follow that I have to appreciate my status altogether as it is, as it happens, and in its reality.

Moreover, I have to be thankful to those who helped in my recovery, in my healing, in my rising to life, in my second life, and in my new situation. I'd like to thank those who gave me treatments, those professionals who supported me, those who encouraged my healing, those whom I care for and in my relations, those who wished me well, and those who prayed for me. It goes without saying that all the above know about my predicaments. They were there to witness when I was sick and had my operations. I was not aware of it, and I will never be aware of it. They suffered the suffering I was not awake to witness.

They experienced the hurt I was not part of. They held the angst I was nowhere to join in. They passed through the consummations I was not part of. That would be my only wondrous luck.

What is relevant, despite the physical pain I experienced, despite my drawbacks, despite my limitations, despite my weaknesses, is to appreciate my situation and those who contributed in making it bearable.

Moreover, this situation may well have relevance to me, changing my life and my thoughts.

A Second Life

When I recovered, the reception assistant in the GP surgery noted to his colleague, 'You remember, this was the guy who had the accident. It was encouraging to hear them say, 'It is another life for you.' It was uncalled for, unexpected, and well meaning. Another life it would be, a second life, a different life, life number two (I spent life number one somehow in some form). My observations, my thinking, and my views of what is around me are all new and different. It looks much further, a few years further than when I would first recognize it physically. Nothing is as I thought I knew it, as I interpreted it, or as I concluded it before, considering I have.

This is not a second-level promotion; this is not a transfer or a move across. This is not a change from one to another. This is not a choice, a decision, or a move of courage. It is what it is—an encounter, a happening, a configuration, a confluence. What makes it unlucky is that it is not chosen or achieved with ease. What makes it lucky is that it should come about after some total withdrawal or death and a rebirth, and that is not how it occurred. It just happened. It was distinctly somehow a rise, and it makes me wonder how it feels to Christ in flesh, rising in three days, according to the Christian scriptures.

Nevertheless, what is more relevant is how it is conducted, how it transpires, how it is run, how it is experienced, and how it is undertaken. That is to say how I undertake it, how I use it, and how I engage in it. That remains to be my challenge, an extensive challenge it is.

Much of the advice that I will need and will continue to need, apart from how I should manage my current health, is how I should undertake any manoeuvres to improve my new life and how I should achieve a positive outcome to the challenges stated above.

Me in My Second Life

*I*t sounds odd to talk about a new world, but that is how it looks to me in this context. After all, when the world was created, it continued transforming—call it developing or changing in time—and this is not a process of a short time. On my return, I found it different or I did not fit in to it, considering that it couldn't have been a lifetime, although my mind was set on that belief.

The time I spent in the hospitals (a few months perhaps) indicated that my brain stopped functioning and mind capacity was totally halted. In the hospitals, I had to learn the basics, such as my name and my date of birth. I had to go through extensive processes of learning words and sentences and exercising what the furniture in front of me were called. Now that my logical mindset is waking up, one thing is certain—when I first started school, I am certain I qualified and passed with flying colours when asked what my name was and my age. It was a basic requirement to be allowed to preschool to further pick up and learn the ABC and 1, 2, 3.

I have improved my thinking capacity, and I am able to write this today as I am reawakened and reinvigorated.

However, my circumstances then damned me to a level below when I was in zero class. A while later, I found myself confused when I said hello to my visitors. My eyes and my brain perfectly identified them, but I could not utter their names or their linkages or what I knew about them. My doubt went like, 'I know and you know that I know you well, but . . .' Fortunately, my visitors seemingly had been inducted and introduced to my mind level, and they seemed perfectly aware of it. They took the confusion as okay, and they accepted it, which bizarrely confused me furthermore. How could I not know their names? And how could they be all right and not be surprised about it? Nevertheless, confusion such as these and others were my staple even when I left the hospital.

Even my neighbours seemed acquainted with the fact that I was not able to work out this and that as my brain was damaged. One neighbour whom I did not recognize and who started chatting bizarrely said that the estate I came back to was built a year ago, considering that I lived in the same estate before I lived in the hospital. I missed the point that I was there before. More likely they were later arrivals. Many such contradictory remarks were heard from my relatives and acquaintances too, suggesting that I forgot a lot of things.

Causes

As I wrote this, I had no inclination, understanding, or make-up of my body system as such, but I could see that I had no leg, no eye, and my concept and understanding of what I see were new and different, including the things provided to me as usually belonging to me. Despite the feeling of attachment from them being lost, for example, I am able to remember the concept and figure out that a jumper is meant to be worn on top, pockets are used for carrying small articles, buttons are used to fasten a garment. I feel I have lost the attachment to or liking for my shirt or jumper, for example.

I have a vague memory of about four months ago from today. It was my last memory while in the first hospital. It was two months after I was admitted at the first hospital in the first place.

While on a wheelchair being pushed across the corridor to the toilets by a nurse, as my understanding now tells me, a junior doctor courteously stated directly to me, 'I was there when you were in intensive care, and you look very well and strong now.' Furthermore, a visiting elder told me that I am very lucky that I came out of it alive. Off the episode, the capacity of my thinking and analysis was so slim, but I got the thinking blurred analysis that went like, 'I lost a leg, and that is a good result?'

Around that time, I found out that my body had lost a leg. One evening, one of my toes was itchy, apparently a toe in my lost leg. My mind presided to ask myself, 'I have no leg, and so no toe, so how come I have an itchy toe?' I got up, looked at my lying half leg to prove my thinking, and argued with myself not to respond to the call of scratching and went back to lying. Some minutes later, I believe I got the urge of the attention-seeking phantom toe and found myself responding to the call by scratching my stump end, the protruding end piece of the leg, which by this time was healed and not patched or covered in any form.

You will agree with me that a lost leg or body part would have some sort of wound, dripping blood, some pain, and possibly patch cloth, wool, cotton covers to the healing wound. I saw or experienced none of these on my lost leg. This may be considered a lucky or an unlucky event. Any argument that will come across hinting that it was seen magically flying into the skies has my vote as the nearest possibility I am inclined to believe.

What Helped? Saved by the Common Person

*I*f all was left to what one can get from medicine and hospitals, it wouldn't go a couple of steps forward.

Originating from a family tree with God's fear and from a community bound by God's belief, my body or living self found itself pursued and assisted by people of the community at every stage. Their assistance and encouragement to my immediate family and their sacrifices and dedication are a debt that I cannot return. And all that goes without knowing anything, seen nothing but from the feelings that pursue.

One passed a note, saying, 'When God takes something from your grasp, he's not hurting you but merely opening your hands to receive something else. The will of God will never take you where the grace of God will not protect you.'

Another person passed another note saying that my strength may no longer return to how it was before the incident or injury, but I must see and focus on the blessing of the new reality of my life. The old me as I knew him had gone, but there is now the new one, whom I need to nurture.

I have spent almost two years in hospitals When I was dispatched to the second hospital with an amputated leg, brain damage, a lost eye, and other medical drawbacks, I felt the encouragement and support from my community members, relatives, and friends. In addition to the treatments, this helped me cope and recover. Moreover, as I wrote this, it was only known to the community people and medical people, and despite having totally lost my memory about what befell on me, I couldn't help but appreciate my life when I woke up four months down the line.

I had never known the value of the community, and this was until I found myself with these medical drawbacks.

Although it was a new encounter to me nearly a year later, the fact remains that my relatives and community people witnessed my medical condition seven or so months before now, before I started to understand them, when I was starting to get the gist of it all. They saw wounds which most luckily I did not see, and they felt the pain which I did not feel. It gave me the idea or concept of where dead people tend to go, leaving those who are alive to bear the feeling of loss. I am not positioned to say I suffered or I was hurt when I was being treated in the hospital. That was until I was healed and discharged from the hospital.

My Takes

My take is rather irrelevant, considering that my awareness is rather limited for the best part if not none. There is logic in recounting a story. For example, being limbless is preceded by some sort of a wound as a result of the accident or operation. Nevertheless, there would be the flesh, bone, blood that would be dissected, or there would be a patchwork to cover the wound from the operation.

As for me, I have none of that. I witnessed or felt none of that kind. I have not seen a wound. I have not seen a patch. I have not had to be careful around a wound. I have not felt pain from a fresh wound. I have not seen any indicators of these nor felt any of these.

How should I feel about it all now? When I try to recount what happened to me, it brings forward different opinions. There are those who feel I am a lucky person. There are those who say, 'How fortunate of you not to witness any pain. It's miraculous.' There are those who think, 'How unfortunate of you to lose your memory.' There are those who say, 'Poor loved ones, they cannot ask what happened to you.' And there are those who observe, 'How complex and unwarranted.'

Two months after I was admitted to the first hospital, I began to be aware of what happened to me. I picked up from the statements made about me that I had been in a coma for two weeks. In my third month, I began seeing some of the people that I knew well. I found myself stating to them that I knew them well, but their names, their roles, and their partners would skip my mind.

I was then told that I would be going to a second hospital. It was a limb hospital and a rehab centre near a place I know. I only knew that it would provide me an artificial leg. My sense of geography was not able to decipher where that place was or anywhere else that I knew before the accident. What a rehab meant was not something my mind was able to decipher.

The things that had been modes of my life and identity were concentrated by physiotherapy, speech therapy, occupational therapy, and neuropsychology.

Physiotherapy was done to measure the development of my new to be leg, teaching and practising me to stand, to use sticks, and to walk, as well as monitoring the strength of my leg and body.

Speech therapy had started from the other hospital, teaching and practising me to say my name and know my date of birth. Later on, it continued to monitor and test my ability to read and to remember a sentence and topic in the other hospital.

Occupational therapy was meant to provide me introduction to life skills, starting from the very basic things, like how to sign a form and make a cup of coffee. It was also meant to assess my capabilities and weaknesses.

Neuropsychology was an ongoing process to determine my thought processes, feelings, and interpretations to know how the brain damage has affected my capabilities. I found myself finding and interpreting most things to be oddly aligned towards me in all aspects.

My Take Then and Now

As I wrote this, I was being discharged from the hospital, and I felt I was being admitted to the first hospital once again. You would expect that a release from the hospital would be the gathering of health, but not for me. For me, it felt like the hospital is where I have spent 99 per cent of my life and it is where I belong, despite the fact that the reality is otherwise. Hence, it left the question, 'Why am I not excited to leave the hospital?' The reason is not that I had exciting times in the hospital, that I was treated favourably, or that my life outside the hospital is damned. It just happened that my sentiment failed to recognize and connect to life outside the hospital or perhaps life itself.

This is due to the fact that my presence in the hospitals previously only affected, disturbed, and manoeuvred people who cared for me and my relatives. As for now, being discharged to the home that my previous self is acquainted with is the time when I began to absorb the experience I had gone through—the loss of a limb, brain damage, and other illnesses that befell me.

Being given the green light forward, I was released from the rehab hospital after spending four months there.

Perspectives of Heaven

Final Training

I was listed and invited to attend a patient discussion group meeting in the dining room. Attendees were encouraged to tell a story or recount their views. As my communication skills were very minimal initially, I found it difficult to share my views and opinions or tell a story. I found it interesting to know that my uptake was virtually removed from what I knew about and thought of. I became more of a spectator and a listener, but I was interested. My speech therapist provided me some stories to read. I would make notes and then present them to her. This was helpful, and after a few weeks, I found myself being able to present them with less attention to the notes I wrote.

In these events, I remember that various patients were to discuss and present their views as to where the World Cup should be held in 2018. Many patients made valid arguments on where they think it should be held. I found myself joining the group that opted for Russia. My simple reason was that I would be able to cope with the rush of things, being a slow walker.

After a couple of months, I started therapy in the new specialist hospital. I was given a practice bus ride to a supermarket with an occupational therapist and physiotherapist.

Memory Loss

I have no idea, but what I know now is that a child before attending preschool would be conversant with knowing one's name, age, and date of birth. 'What is your name?' asked the speech therapist casually. Looking at my struggle perhaps, the therapist continued to suggest, 'Yo . . . Yosief, isn't it? What is your date of birth?' The therapist possibly noted the confusion in my head. 'Twenty-two . . . Two . . .' I repeated after. 'Nineteen seventy.' I repeated it. 'Well done' is the credit I get, possibly for being able to repeat—if not, what else?

I clearly remember that there was a particular doctor during the visit around the patients' beds. When he would arrive at my bed, he would always throw a question. These were questions such as 'What is your name?' and 'How old are you?' Now it seems to me that he was testing my memory comeback.

Lacking the basic levels of knowing my name and date of birth, I should be excused for being unable to remember, recognize, or repeat the names of persons that came to see me. I confidently knew who they were; I just couldn't work out their names, their jobs, or other facts about them.

Taken on a short bus trip for the first time, I was not sure what I missed or picked up, but I knew how to get on the bus, whose driver was instructed in detail by the occupational therapist in front of me. A week later, the same trip reveals a few things that I was aware of, like the type of buildings and road instructions. 'I know this place. It is England.' Anyone will convince me, saying that the previous week on the bus, I was in Timbuktu, Frankfurt, Eritrea, or South Africa.

I couldn't follow the story of a programme on TV. I couldn't read a paragraph of a book. I found it helpful to read short-paragraphed self-help books.

My episode under the influence of the sickness—if I can call it that as it is not something that would elapse at any time—was followed by times and events that were challenging and odd. When I was released after my treatment at the hospitals, I found myself being at odds with everything around me. I felt the world around me belittling me and distancing from me.

What I see and what I sense is, things that I see and hear are those ten years beyond where I am or what my capacity can notice. It seemed like I spent ten years in the hospital despite the fact that I was told that I stayed there for only around three year. I couldn't explain the happenings around me. It seems to me that I have to adapt, stop questioning, and accept it. To some extent, this challenges me, and my psyche and brain are victims of my sickness also.

They are odd. Why they happen, I have no idea, but to date, I have not got any memory of what befell me. What I know is that I had a glance at eternity.

About the Author

*B*orn on 05 April 1964 in Eritrea in northeast Africa, Yosief Tewolde Zerezghi is a son of a construction truck driver, the late Tewolde Zerezghi, and a housewife, Roshan Ekub. Yosief has one brother, who died in the war between Eritrea and Ethiopia, and three elder sisters.

Yosief studied primary school at St Joseph's in Keren (today's Eritrea) and secondary school in the capital city Asmara.

He joined a religious organisation called Christian Brothers, where he continued following his secondary school. When he reached the working age, he was assigned by the organisation to attend his career training in Ethiopia. Subsequently, he was assigned to teach in Eritrea and Ethiopia.

Considering the bad political situation under Ethiopia, he moved to the United Kingdom in 1989 as a refugee fleeing the conflict that was taking place in Eritrea. He went to university and achieved a degree in chemical engineering and a master's degree in environmental science. Yosief worked in various organisations as a process engineer, safety officer, and safety engineer.

Yosief had an active life that went bizarrely to a different direction, following a drastic accident that involved a train. The major results of the accident were brain damage, amputation, and blindness in one eye.

Yosief spent a lengthy time in different hospitals and rehabilitation centres. Considering that he had to be trained to learn the basics, like his name and date of birth, the current status and situation is grossly amazing to him and those who followed him closely.

It is this great achievement that the book narrates. Whether you want to see it as a self-help and self-confidence-building story or you want to follow an amazing story, this is for you

Index

A

accident   7, 20, 37
amputatation   4, 6, 27, 37
appreciation   19

B

birth   10, 23, 30, 34, 38
brain damage   4, 7, 13, 27, 30-1, 37
brain trauma   7

C

comatose   5-7, 9, 29
confusion   6, 24, 34

D

death   20
depression   15
disabilities   4, 6, 18-19

E

encouragement   11, 27-8
Enya   19
eternity   1, 3-4, 6, 9, 35

G

Glaucoma   4

H

heaven   33
hospital   1, 4-6, 10-11, 13-14, 17,
         23-5, 27-31, 33, 35, 38

L

limitations   18, 20

M

memory   5-7, 10-11, 28-9, 35

memory loss   34

mental illness   15

N

neuropsychology   30

P

pain   6-7, 9, 26, 28-9

perspective   6, 17, 33

physiotherapy   13-14, 30, 33

R

rehabilitation   4, 15, 17, 30-1, 38

S

specialist hospital   33

speech therapist   10, 14, 33-4

suicide   15

T

therapist   14, 34

  occupational   14

W

wounds   5-6, 26, 28-9

CPSIA information can be obtained
at www.ICGtesting.com
Printed in the USA
BVHW080237110119
537596BV00001B/138/P

9 781514 460627